Gone Too Soon:
Deaths That Changed Wrestling
by Ian Hamilton

www.theianhamilton.com
www.facebook.com/ianhamiltonbooks

In memory of

Adam Firestorm
(Adam T. Dykes)

1976-2009

Introduction

As a form of entertainment, professional wrestling has been around for years. Whether it was the early 1900s, the era of the territories, or the modern-day period of global superstars, fans have been paying their money to watch shows and to back "their" man. Whether that was Frank Gotch in the 1900s, Lou Thesz in the post-war era, or even the modern day stars such as Hulk Hogan, Ric Flair and John Cena, every card had someone you wanted to win.

Regardless of when you started watching, whether you believed it was 100% real or not, the chances are that you'll have sat through a lot of matches, plenty of storylines featuring numerous different performers. The highs of watching your favourite wrestlers winning titles, the excitement of (well written) storylines, and the angst caused by watching shows that don't live up to expectations. But hey, that's life, right?

Away from the cameras, though, another part of the real world impinges into the "fake" world of professional wrestling all too often: death. It's a natural part of life. So is change, and throughout life, it's only natural for the death of those around you to change your outlook on life. But how does the wrestling world react to these deaths?

Known as "the call", it's something that was happening far too often in the late 90s/early 2000s, and something that was rightly feared. A telephone call from a close friend or colleague telling you that someone you knew had passed on. Sadly, as time goes on, and the wrestling world gets more and more acclimated to these deaths, the passing of someone who may have been your hero goes from being headline news to a story that gets barely a passing mention in the wrestling world.

Having been a fan of wrestling since the early 90s, I've lived through a period where a lot of the guys I grew up watching on TV have passed on. I suppose you could say that it's reached a point where, apart from the most extreme cases, the news of another wrestler dying barely registers with me anymore - to paraphrase Taz's old catchphrase, "just another victim" of the wrestling industry. Most of these deaths are defined as the stereotypical "wrestler's death" - the after-effects of years of taking steroids and other performance enhancing substances, typically ending in heart failure.

So often, whenever a wrestler dies, it's not been a shock. For the most part, the years spent watching their enhanced bodies would have given you the tip-off as to their grim future. Although there are cases where former stars pass away through old age or natural causes, or in even rarer cases, as a result of a wrestling move gone wrong, the majority of deaths neatly fall into the aforementioned pile of "wrestler's deaths". As very few of these deaths happened to wrestlers who were actively under contract to one of the major promotions (WWE especially), it's so easy to sweep these under the carpet and say that their behaviour was nothing to do with the company.

However, there are those rare times when the death isn't to someone who made their name years ago and was living off of former glories. There are times when the deceased was still a household name and appearing weekly on television. Those are often the times when a death sends shockwaves amongst those who knew them, whether it's as a friend, a colleague, an acquaintance or simply as a fan... and amongst those times, there becomes a moment when everyone comes together to force through change, almost as if everyone agrees that "something has to be done".

This book isn't an attempt to "rank" the deaths of wrestlers in any way, or indeed, to eulogise over performers who left us many years ago. To do so, especially having experienced a wrestler's death both as a fan and as a friend, would be trivial. Instead, this book hopes to characterise the lives and careers of three men who made their living through professional wrestling, and the way in which their untimely demise changed their profession - for good or for bad.

In the space of a little over eight years, there were three deaths in wrestling which shook the industry to its core, all of which resulted in major changes to the industry itself. But if you were to have asked them, in life, whether the legacy they left to the industry was what they actually left behind, none of them would have wanted it to have happened the way it did.

Note: throughout this book, and for ease of reference, I shall be referring to companies under their current-day monikers. So, whilst I may be referring to the "World Wrestling Federation" for anything pre-2002, acronym-wise, I'll always be referring to it as "WWE".

OWEN HART

(May 7, 1965 - May 23, 1999)

Growing up as the son of a legendary Canadian wrestler can't be easy. As the 12th, and final, child of Hall of Famer Stu Hart, Owen was meant to be the only one of Stu's eight sons to avoid any sort of involvement in professional wrestling. In truth, you could say that he'd tried all he could to avoid going into the sport, limiting his grappling experience to amateur wrestling whilst he was at high school in Calgary and setting his heart on a career as a fire fighter..

Although Owen tried to forge a life for himself outside of wrestling, it didn't take too long for the family business to creep into his life, as Owen ended up working for his family's Stampede Wrestling promotion, which was initially created and run by Stu Hart. By the time Owen had taken his first steps into the professional game, Stampede Wrestling was a company that was just a glowing ember compared to the burning fires of their heyday. After having been bought out by the WWE's Vince McMahon in 1984, Bruce Hart (Stu's second son) reformed the company in 1985. As a Hart, Owen was one of the main stars in the reformed promotion, a promotion whose second wind barely lasted four years, and probably wasn't helped by their blossoming star wrestling around the world.

Touring the globe, Owen performed for the New Japan Pro Wrestling promotion, taking on such stars as Ultimo Dragon, the Pegasus Kid (Chris Benoit) and Keiichi Yamada - both with and without a mask (Yamada would gain worldwide fame under the mask as Jushin "Thunder" Liger). Another country graced by Owen Hart's early work was the United Kingdom, where Owen appeared on the now-classic "World of Sport" wrestling shows, with his March 1987 match against Marty Jones becoming a gem that has since been unearthed thanks to the modern-day wonder that is YouTube.

With the promise of WWE's riches, Owen Hart arrived in the company in late 1988 and quickly discovered that he wasn't going to wrestle under his real name. Since his elder brother Bret was starting to make a name for himself as a singles wrestler, the decision was made to not confuse fans by promoting two Hart brothers at the opposite end of the card. The younger Hart would be given a whole new character. Initially debuting in Los Angeles as the "Blue Angel" - a take on the Los Angeles Angels baseball team - Owen would later see his character's name altered to a less identifiable "Blue Blazer". The character would see Owen Hart run down to the ring in a blue mask, blue pants and a blue cape.

Wrestling under a mask was nothing new for Owen, as he had been masked very early on in his wrestling career in a move that allowed him to wrestle on a professional level whilst remaining anonymous - and more importantly, eligible for the high school wrestling team! Unfortunately for Owen, the Blue Blazer character didn't get much play in a late 80s scene that was dominated by muscle-bound wrestlers, and barely six months after debuting, having made two losing pay-per-view appearances at the Survivor Series, and a loss to Mr. Perfect (Curt Hennig) at WrestleMania V, Owen chose to leave the WWE to try his luck elsewhere.

Elsewhere turned out to be a return to Stampede Wrestling, which was limping along following it's "revival" by Bruce Hart. Back on his old stomping grounds, the idea was that Owen's mainstream exposure would draw new fans to Stampede's product. This didn't quite work, although Owen remained a big star in Stampede until the promotion closed its doors at the end of 1989. Further worldwide appearances followed, as Owen padded out his diary with shows whilst wrestling under his real name and under the mask of the Blue Blazer. Nowadays, that would simply not happen, as WWE would likely have flattened any promotion with cease and desist warnings that even dared to promote a show using one of "their" characters. Owen would go on to have a brief flirtation with the WWE's biggest rival - WCW - perhaps foreshadowing the move his brother would make there many years later. Owen would appear on WCW's syndicated shows, but this would not turn into anything more permanent.

With the Blue Blazer gimmick still a figurative monkey on Owen's back, the character was put to rest in Mexico, as a result of a mask vs. mask match in Naucalpan in May 1991 for the now-defunct Universal Wrestling Association. Following the short match, the Blue Blazer was unmasked and paraded to the crowd as Owen Hart, which freed him up for a return to the North American mainstream. As WCW hemmed and hawed over a contract, the WWE swooped to re-sign the youngest Hart, this time opting to promote him sans gimmick. Instead, Owen would be placed into a tag team.

In the world of wrestling, the word "new" is virtually a kiss of death, especially when it comes to tag teams in the 1990s. Owen turned out to be one of the victims of a reconditioned tag team name, as his first assignment back with the WWE was with his brother's former tag team partner, Jim "The Anvil" Neidhart , forming "The New Foundation". Having been at a loose end since the Hart Foundation briefly re-formed and split in 1990, Neidhart was rescued from being a colour commentator and was thrown back into competition with his real-life brother-in-law. This team made only one pay-per-view appearance, albeit in the days when WWE only held four pay-per-views a year, with their sole appearance being a win over the Orient Express, as Neidhart left the WWE under acrimonious circumstances, jumping ship to the rival WCW promotion.

Owen, having committed himself to a WWE contract, didn't have a choice, and remained in tag team competition where he was placed into a team with long-time preliminary act Koko B. Ware (and his bird, Frankie). The pair donned MC Hammer-esque baggy pants to become "High Energy". The team didn't get much success, with a loss to the Headshrinkers at the 1992 Survivor Series being the duo's sole pay-per-view appearance, before the people in charge at the WWE opted to take Owen out of the tag team ranks and focus on him as a singles wrestler. Or at least, that was the plan, as much of 1993 was spent preparing him for a big run as a heel - Owen spent a large part of the year backing his brother Bret in an ongoing feud with Jerry "The King" Lawler, which was meant to culminate in a match at the 1993 Survivor Series, with the Hart Family taking on Jerry Lawler and his masked knights.

As legal issues ruled Lawler out of the show, the match went ahead with the distinctly un-regal Shawn Michaels and his knights taking on the Harts - a match which served only to build up to its ending (the way all matches should be!). After having lost all of his hired knights, Michaels managed to eliminate Owen from the match after Owen accidentally collided into Bret, giving Michaels enough time to get a school-boy roll-up for the pin. Shawn would later eliminate himself by count-out, resulting in the match ending and causing the Hart Family to celebrate... minus Owen. He would return to join the celebrations, only to prompt an on-screen bust-up that served to plant the seeds for the following year's storyline.

In the immediate aftermath of this, yet another tag team was in Owen's future, as he tagged with his brother Bret for a tag team title shot at January 1994's Royal Rumble against the Quebecers (a pro-French-Canadian tag team, made up of Pierre Oulette and Jacques Rougeau - better known as "The Mountie"). Appearing to patch up their differences, it would seem that the Hart Brothers would win the tag team titles, only for Bret to pick up a storyline knee injury that would prevent a fresher, healthy Owen from being tagged in. The injury would see the match end, as the referee deemed Bret "unable to continue", before awarding the match to the Quebecers. After the match, Owen attacked Bret's injured leg, before walking out on him. As Bret was helped to the back, Owen appeared on the video screen in the arena, bragging about "kicking (Bret's) leg out of his leg" before berating his brother for being "selfish"... and so began arguably the biggest year of Owen's wrestling career.

Although Bret lost out on the WWE tag team titles, he did end up being a joint winner of the Royal Rumble on the same night, with both Bret and Lex Luger ruling to have eliminated each other at exactly the same time. With the winner of the Royal Rumble getting a WWE title shot, Bret was to wrestle a match to ensure that he did not have an unfair advantage ahead of his opportunity. Bret's first match at WrestleMania X, would be against his brother, Owen, in the first match of that year's show - a match, which Owen would claim an upset win with a blocked victory roll, as he later saw his brother win the WWE title by pinning Yokozuna in the main event.

Perhaps spurred on by his brother's success, Owen would go on a run that somewhat mirrored Bret's - first winning that year's King of the Ring tournament with victories over Tatanka and the 1-2-3 Kid, before capping it off with a victory over Razor Ramon in the finals. That victory in the finals was helped by a returning Jim "The Anvil" Neidhart - whose interference had been responsible for Bret Hart's disqualification loss to Diesel earlier in the show. The former "New Foundation" were reunited, but the tournament victory would give Owen a nickname that stuck for the rest of his career; a nickname perhaps inspired by a certain beer: The King of Harts. Having won the tournament, Owen was now placed in a prime spot for a summer-long feud with his brother over the WWE title, although whatever advantage Owen had with having Jim Neidhart in his corner was negated by the return of another member of the extended Hart family, as the "British Bulldog" made his WWE return, aligning himself with the "Hitman".

After losing a stellar cage match at SummerSlam in 1994, Owen would prove to be the deciding factor in

Bret's title run coming to an end, during a submissions match at the Survivor Series show in November 1994. The match saw Bret defending against a former WWE champion from the 80s, Bob Backlund, with the match only ending with one of the combatants either giving up, or having the towel thrown in for them. Each man had a wrestler in their corner - Bret had the British Bulldog in his corner, whilst Backlund was cornered by Owen, with the rest of the Hart family present for the event in San Antonio, Texas. During the match, Bret's corner man, the British Bulldog, ended up being "knocked out" after colliding with the steel ring steps. As Bret was distracted by the Bulldog's bump, Backlund snuck behind the champion and applied his finishing move, the cross-face chicken wing. Unable to submit, or have the towel thrown in for him, Owen suddenly started to appear concerned for his brother's safety, and started to plead for his mother, Helen, to throw the towel in. Eventually, Helen relented, and threw in the towel that had been held by the downed British Bulldog, therefore ending the match... and quickly revealing that Owen's concern was phoney, as he celebrated the loss of his brother's WWE title.

The Bret vs. Owen feud would continue for a few more months - Owen would play a part in Bret's title shot with then-champion Diesel (aka Kevin Nash, who had beaten Bob Backlund for the title, just days after the 1994 Survivor Series in a match that lasted just eight seconds), as the match ended a no-contest when both Bret and Diesel were attacked during the match. Owen would go on to enter the Royal Rumble match itself, but barely made any impact, as he was quickly dispatched by the British Bulldog, ending any dreams that Owen may have had of holding the WWE title.

As the family feud was put to one side, Owen went back to becoming something of a tag team specialist, winning the WWE tag team titles at WrestleMania XI, with mystery partner Yokozuna joining Owen to dethrone the Smoking Gunns (Billy and Bart). The remainder of 1995 would largely be spent holding the belts, before the belts were lost in a multiple-belt match at September's In Your House event, as WWE champion Diesel and Intercontinental champion Shawn Michaels took on the tag team champions (the rules stated that if Diesel or Shawn lost, their title would go to whomever pinned them). The British Bulldog filled in for Owen Hart, who was supposedly given the night off to be present for the birth of his daughter Athena - although Owen ran in to interfere in the match (and ultimately get pinned), the fact that he wasn't meant to be in the match resulted in the titles reverting back to Owen and Yokozuna... albeit for 24 hours, as they promptly lost the belts back to the Smoking Gunns on the following night's taping of Raw.

Owen would regain the tag team titles a year later, this time as part of a team with the British Bulldog in what would be a precursor to the rebirth of the Hart Foundation in 1997. In the meantime though, the team of Owen and the Bulldog would have the typical "tag team falling out", with dissension between the two which culminated in their match against each other in the finals of a tournament to crown the first ever WWE European Champion at a show in Berlin, Germany in February 1997. Still holding on to the tag team titles, Owen and the Bulldog would have a mini-feud over the new European title - a feud that would end with a massive family reunion.

As Owen and the Bulldog were in the middle of a match against each other, Bret Hart came to the ring and talked the two out of their ongoing woes, blaming America for turning family against each other, and forming the new Hart Foundation. Instead of the tag team that we saw in the 80s, the 90s' version of the Hart Foundation was a five man stable, with Bret and Owen Hart being joined by brother in laws Jim "The Anvil" Neidhart and the British Bulldog, whilst family friend (and trainee of the famous Hart family Dungeon) Brian Pillman completing the quintet.

Early on in the Hart Foundation's run, Owen had skirmishes from two of the hottest stars of the modern era. Initially winning the Intercontinental title from Rocky Maivia (best known as The Rock), Owen would then take on another of the era's biggest names: Stone Cold Steve Austin. Initially dropping the tag team titles to the team of Shawn Michaels and Stone Cold, Owen and the Bulldog regained the titles, only to lose them to Austin and his new partner, Dude Love (aka Mick Foley). Austin would go on to capture Owen's Intercontinental title at SummerSlam 1997, in a match that would become famous for shortening, if not nearly ending, Austin's career. As the title match reached its climax, Owen went to give Austin a sit-out tombstone piledriver - a move that wasn't exactly performed regularly by Owen. By accident, Austin's head was positioned too low down, and the impact of the move resulted in temporary paralysis for "Stone Cold". Realising something was wrong, Owen stalled for time, as Austin managed to clamber onto his knees to deliver the world's worst schoolboy roll-up to win the match and the Intercontinental title.

As Austin took time off to recover from the broken neck, the WWE creative team decided to turn a real life accident into a storyline, with Owen mocking Austin's fate, spoofing his trademark "Austin 3:16" t-shirt with his own "Owen 3:16" shirts, and a catchphrase of "Owen 3:16 says I just broke your neck." Owen would go on to win a tournament for the vacated Intercontinental title, beating Faarooq (Ron Simmons) in the final, thanks to some help from Austin, who would explain his interference by saying he only wanted to regain the title from Owen. Austin would defeat Owen for the title at the 1997 Survivor Series, but it would be the aftermath of that night's main event that would redefine Owen's WWE career.

Known as the "Montreal Screwjob", the main event of the 1997 Survivor Series was remembered for much more than Bret Hart losing the WWE title to Shawn

Michaels. In the weeks prior to the match, Bret had been informally asked to walk out of the WWE and seek employment with the rival WCW promotion, despite Bret having been tied to a twenty-year, multi-million-dollar contract with the WWE. As Bret reached an agreement with WCW, there was the issue of just what would happen with Bret's WWE title - coming into the Survivor Series, Bret remained the champion, but with rumours gathering pace that WCW would announce Bret's signing the following night, it seemed that something had to give.

The events of November 9, 1997 are discussed to this very day, mostly thanks to numerous repeat performances by various wrestling promotions, but the end result saw Bret Hart leave the WWE for WCW. Out of the remaining members of the Hart Foundation (Brian Pillman had passed away a month earlier, being found dead in a motel room in Minnesota prior to a WWE pay-per-view), Owen was the only one who was refused a contract release: both the British Bulldog and Jim Neidhart were able to buy themselves out of their contract and headed for WCW, whilst WWE refused Owen's every effort to join his brother.

Owen eventually returned to WWE television by the end of 1997, Owen attacked Shawn Michaels at the end of the D-Generation X pay-per-view, after Shawn had successfully defended the title against Ken Shamrock. Sporting a new character, "The Black Hart" was now a fan favourite, riding on the pro-Hart-family sentiment generated by the events of Montreal. He quickly gained singles gold, albeit in nonsensical fashion (beating a Triple H-impersonating Goldust to win Triple H's European title). Various backstage politics meant that a planned feud between Owen Hart and Shawn Michaels - for Michaels' WWE title - was downgraded, perhaps on the theory that Owen wasn't established as a main eventer, and as such was deemed too big a risk to be in the main event.

Of course, the "other" theory made just as much sense - that Owen may have been ready to give Shawn a "receipt" or two for what happened at Montreal, and not be as co-operative in the match as he would like. As a result, Shawn's replacement in the feud was his D-Generation X stable mate, and future-man-in-charge-of-WWE, Triple H. It was at this point that Owen was given a rather derogatory nickname, which wasn't as easy to promote as "The Rocket" or "The King of Harts". Owen's new nickname, at least from the edgy-heel DX, was the "Nugget", supposedly because DX (in storyline) had flushed all of the Hart family out of WWE, and, comparing the Harts to human waste, Owen was the last "nugget" left. Perhaps comparing WWE to a toilet wasn't the smartest idea, but nevertheless, it resulted in whatever popularity Owen had as a babyface waning away pretty quickly, and as a result, the feud with Triple H was short lived. Owen would go back to his familiar ways, turning heel, as he joined yet another faction: the Nation of Domination.

As a white Canadian, Hart seemed somewhat out of place in a group that was intended to be a take on the "black power" group of the same name, Owen was lofted to "joint leader" of the Nation, alongside the Rock. However, as the D-Generation X stable was promoted ahead of the Nation, Owen found himself sidelined once again, with a series of matches against Ken Shamrock being the only bright point as we approached the summer of 1998. Another change of pace saw Owen being shifted into yet-another-tag-team, this time with a man who would attempt to shape the future of wrestling just four short years later (when he created the TNA promotion) - Jeff Jarrett.

Owen's team was pretty much thrown together during a time where WWE had bigger priorities than their tag team division. With previous champions such as Kane, Mankind, Steve Austin, and even the tag team stalwarts of the New Age Outlaws - of the Road Dogg and "Bad Ass" Billy Gunn - carving out careers for themselves in the singles division, it was fair to say that tag team wrestling was an afterthought by this point. So much so, indeed, that aside from their WrestleMania outing - a tag team title defence against pre-show battle royal winners Test and D'Lo Brown - the legacy of the Owen and Jarrett team would end up being something that never happened.

By 1999, the WWE was a far different company than the one that Owen Hart had initially joined in the late

80s. Gone were the days of slow paced matches and simplistic storylines - the Montreal incident had been used as an excuse to replace an old, tired (but admittedly, working) format with a style of television that became known as "crash TV". Most commonly associated with wrestling writer Vince Russo, who had his only fame in WWE in the late 90s, before failing to repeat these successes in WCW and TNA, the format of "crash TV" was, simply put, a translation of the saying "throw everything against the wall and see what sticks". Characters, instead of being amplified versions of a wrestler's real personas, would become sensationalised, and shows would often end up resembling episodes of Jerry Springer inside a wrestling ring. Owen was given a storyline and quickly shot it down.

Perhaps intended as a way to break-up his current partnership with Jeff Jarrett, Owen was to have developed a fixation for his team's buxom manager, Debra, which was to have caused friction between Owen and Jeff. In real life, Debra had been married to former NFL defensive tackle Steve "Mongo" McMichael, which was in some way responsible for her breaking into wrestling, initially with WCW, before jumping to WWE (as Jeff Jarrett's manager) following her divorce. Debra would go on to marry "Stone Cold" Steve Austin; a marriage that ended in a somewhat acrimonious divorce.

Taking into account the feelings of his wife (his childhood sweetheart, Martha) and their two young children, Owen shot down this storyline out of hand, which left his tag team with Jeff Jarrett in something of a holding pattern. Management didn't want to split up the team for no reason, but without a long term storyline, there was no point in their existence. At the end of 1998, Owen retired in a storyline where he had supposedly injured UFC fighter-turned-wrestler Dan "The Beast" Severn following a piledriver. Unfortunately, this storyline didn't resonate with fans anywhere near as much as the legitimate injury with Steve Austin did the previous year, but the storyline did what it was meant to do - it wrote out Owen Hart and put his team with Jeff Jarrett on ice, allowing the WWE to go back to the past yet again for Owen Hart's latest reinvention. He would once again don the blue mask and singlet, and go back to a character that had been consigned to history... or so we thought. However, it would be the rekindling of a character which would eventually be the end of Owen Hart.

This version of the Blue Blazer character was nothing like the bland masked hero who first burst onto our screens in the late 80s. This Blue Blazer was an anti-anti-hero, disgusted with his surroundings in the somewhat seedy Attitude era of the WWE, whilst also being portrayed as a bumbling superhero. Although there were comedic aspects to the character, such as the whole "is Owen Hart the Blue Blazer", where Owen "proved" he wasn't the Blazer by having other people under the hood - including Jeff Jarrett and former partner Koko B. Ware (you'd have to have been blind not to have noticed or appreciated the comedy of a black man in a mask portraying a white guy in a mask), ultimately, the Blue Blazer was somewhat ashamed to be in the same company alongside characters such as a former porn star (Val Venis) and a pimp (the Godfather).

Come May 1999, the Blue Blazer character was locked in a feud with the aforementioned Godfather, with the Intercontinental title at stake. As a way to enhance the character, the Blue Blazer would be lowered from the rafters of the arena on a cable, in a rip-off/spoof of the entrance that was being used at the time by WCW main eventer Sting. In the weeks that built up to the Over the Edge pay-per-view, the entrance was tried out several times, but for the show itself, there would be an "improvement" added to it. According to the book "Broken Hart" (written by Owen's widow Martha), the original plans for the entrance would be for Owen to have a "mini Blue Blazer" strapped to him for the entrance. That entrance never happened, as a procrastinating Owen skipped out on the pre-show rehearsals, which resulted in the mini Blue Blazer being axed from the line-up... unfortunately, with Owen being scared of the original entrance idea, the planned "descent into the ring" entrance was to go ahead as scheduled.

As the Over The Edge pay-per-view started, Owen got changed into his Blue Blazer attire, minus the mask, before making his way towards the rafters of the Kemper Arena in Kansas City. With cover-alls hiding the distinctive blue of his wrestling costume, Owen headed through the crowd, and climbed up the steps to the top of the arena, before clambering onto a catwalk that was conveniently (for the entrance, at least) directly overhead, some 70 feet above the ring. Moments after a Hardcore title match between Al Snow and Hardcore Holly concluded, a video package played to the arena and to the watching audience at home, recounting the feud between the Blue Blazer and the Godfather.

With everyone being distracted by the video package, a cabled-up Owen stepped out of the catwalk as he prepared to be lowered via the cable-and-harness set-up down to the ring. The planned entrance was to see the Blue Blazer character stop about a foot from the ring, before "struggling" to disconnect himself and take a prat-fall, in line with the comedic, bungling superhero character that was supposedly being portrayed. What actually took place turned out to be something of a watermark in the history of professional wrestling. As the video package came to an end, the harness apparatus went awry, as a quick-release clasp, that was meant to make the pratfall at the end easier to pull off, was accidentally triggered. Whether it was by Owen adjusting his cape, his mask, or even something as simple as a deep breath, the harness gave way, and Owen plunged into the ring, hitting the ropes, before being thrown onto the canvas.

The only inkling that the viewers at home had that something had gone wrong came through commentator Jim Ross, who segued from the video package to a pre-taped interview with the Blue Blazer. Upon returning from that pre-taped segment, all the viewers at home saw for a lengthy spell were shots of the crowd, as WWE went out of their way not to broadcast any shots of the ring, an image of "Good Ol' JR" at the commentary desk gave us all a good idea of what had gone wrong. Owen Hart had fallen from the ceiling of the Kemper Arena.

In the minutes that unfolded, EMTs feverishly worked to try and resuscitate Owen in the middle of the ring, as a decision was made to continue on with the show regardless - a decision that many contest to this day - even after it was revealed, and announced to the television audience by Jim Ross that Owen had died of his injuries (no announcement was made to the live audience in the arena). The first that those who had been watching the show live at the arena knew of Owen's death would have come via that evening's newscasts - this being in the days before the Internet and mobile phones were prevalent, and long before Facebook and Twitter were commonplace. Owen's death made news worldwide, a sign of how popular both Owen Hart and wrestling in general were at the time.

The following night's edition of Raw was rewritten to be a two-hour tribute to Owen Hart, in a show that would become a template for future high profile deaths. Gone were all semblances of storylines and feuds, instead, the show was full of tearful tributes by wrestlers, as everyone struggled to come to terms with their loss. These tributes let the fans peer behind-the-scenes and find out that the person that they were booing in the ring was in reality a really nice, down to earth man - as many of the wrestlers confirmed, whether he was teased for being cheap, or for wanting to spend more time at home to be with his family, there was simply not a bad word that could have been said about him.

Perhaps a sign of the sheer shock that Owen's death caused, the tribute episode of Monday Night Raw drew a Nielsen television rating of 7.2 - making it the highest rated episode in Raw's history. Meanwhile, on "the other show", WCW's Monday Nitro mentioned Owen's passing - which was somewhat obligatory out of respect, and also given that Bret was in the middle of a planned return following a groin injury. Some months later, Bret would wrestle a tribute match for his brother on an episode of Nitro, at the same arena where Owen died, against Chris Benoit.

As this was in the days where Raw was being shown live one week, with the following week's episode having been taped, the show tried to get back to normal just 48 hours after Owen's passing, as a somewhat-regular episode of Raw was taped, with the only mention being made in the storylines being Jeff Jarrett winning the Intercontinental title from the Godfather - a nod to the common belief that Owen was supposed to have won the title as the Blue Blazer - as the rest of the WWE's storylines picked up where they left off.

In the weeks and months that followed, as the story behind Owen's death became clearer, gradual changes were being made to the wrestling product as a whole. As it became clear that there was a malfunction with the harness that Owen was rigged to, the flashy, elaborate entrances that were glorified stunts were watered down and removed from wrestling, or at the very least, were subjected to more stringent safety checks. In WCW, Sting's entrance, which was the inspiration behind the Blue Blazer spoof entrance, was quickly dropped, especially once it became clear that the quick-release equipment used to lower Owen to the ring was so sensitive, it needed less pressure than that needed to pull the trigger on a gun to activate.

As expected, a lawsuit was filed against the WWE and a multitude of defendants, with the main claims being that the stunt and equipment itself was poorly designed and dangerous. The case was settled out of court in November 2000, with the $18m settlement being used to create a charitable foundation in Owen's name. In the wrestling business though, Owen's death did lead to some changes - the elaborate entrances started to disappear, whilst pointless, high-risk stunts that didn't directly figure into matches were removed (of course, this didn't remove needless matches like WCW's "Human

Torch" match, where a stuntman was set on fire and thrown off of a stage... and another match in WCW where a wrestler was power bombed onto the top of an ambulance before sliding off and landing on the arena floor). Barely a year later, the increased safety measures were clearly visible as WCW held their Slamboree pay-per-view at the same Kemper Arena where Owen Hart had died. The end of the show featured a stunt where Mike Awesome would throw Chris Kanyon off of the second level of a triple-tiered steel cage and onto a heavily padded entrance ramp - a stunt that could, in passing, be compared to Mick Foley's infamous fall from the top of the WWE's Hell in a Cell in June 1996, except whereas Kanyon's fall was broken by padding, Foley only hit the wooden announce table seconds before meeting the solid concrete of the arena floor.

In life, Owen Hart was someone who loved what he did, but at the same time, he also loved his family. At the time of his death, Owen was in the process of moving his family into a new home - his and Martha's "dream home" - the results of years of being ribbed for being a penny pincher, saving monies by travelling with other wrestlers, or getting free car rides from trusted fans. However, as the reinvention of the Blue Blazer was intended to give Owen another chance of making serious money in wrestling, his ways meant that he was all but set for life, and able to seriously consider retiring from the sport before reaching his 40th birthday.

The career of Owen Hart would mean that he would be unable to live the life that he wanted. A career that had changed drastically from what he had originally started off doing, and perhaps most tragic of all, his death, in part, came around from trying to protect his family from yet another storyline that would have been forgotten in the months that followed, in a way that his death did not.

EDDIE GUERRERO

(October 9, 1967 - November 13, 2005)

When your whole family is built around the business of professional wrestling, it's hard to avoid it. Like Owen Hart, Eddie Guerrero was the last son of legendary Mexican wrestler Gory Guerrero. With all of Gory's three prior sons, Chavo, Mando and Hector, all having broken into the wrestling business, you can see what was waiting for Eddie as he grew up.

Although promoted as a Mexican, Eddie was actually born and grew up in El Paso, Texas, before going to college in New Mexico. Prior to that, Eddie started off his career performing during the intermissions of his father's wrestling shows, often at the El Paso Coliseum, Eddie's first matches would involve his nephew Chavo Junior.

Eddie's first serious break into the wrestling business would come in Mexico in the early 90s, working for a promotion called AAA. Originally teaming with the son of another Mexican wrestling legend, El Hijo del Santo (translated literally, the son of El Santo), as part of La Pareja Atomica (The Atomic Pair), Eddie would turn heel and form an alliance with an American by the name of Art Barr. Barr had previously wrestled in the North West of America, as well as for WCW, before heading to Mexico - and became the centre piece of a tag team known as La Pareja del Terror (The Pair of Terror). Through time, Guerrero and Barr would remain a tag team, but would adopt the name "Los Gringos Locos" (the Crazy Americans) as part of a group that included, amongst others, Konnan and Louie Spicolli (known then as Madonna's Boyfriend, and later best known under his real name and as WWE's Rad Radford).

It was this team with Barr that would be responsible for Eddie's first exposure in the United States, as they were booked on a pay-per-view that was jointly promoted between WCW and the AAA promotion. La Pareja del Terror were booked in a traditional lucha libre-rules match - best two out of three falls - against Octagon, and Guerrero's former tag team partner, El Hijo del Santo, in a match where the losing team would have to complete a forfeit - Santo and Octagon would lose their masks, whereas Guerrero and Barr would be shaved bald.

The hair vs. mask match was held on a show called "When Worlds Collide" on November 6, 1994, in front of 13,000 fans inside the Los Angeles Sports Arena, and a pay-per-view audience. Art Barr won the first fall with a frog splash, before going on to lose via submission to level things up. Octagon was stretchered out of the match, leaving La Pareja del Terror with a two-on-one advantage. Of course, El Hijo del Santo was never going to be unmasked, especially when he had unfinished business with

Eddie Guerrero - and as luck would have it, Guerrero was beaten by El Hijo del Santo, forcing La Pareja del Terror to shave their heads.

The performances jointly put on by Guerrero and Barr had caught the eyes of all three of the major national promotions in the US. However, despite appearing on a show that was jointly promoted by World Championship Wrestling, WCW didn't jump at the chance to sign either Barr or Guerrero. As the World Wrestling Federation chose not to sign them either, that left Paul Heyman's fledgling Extreme Championship Wrestling (ECW) group as the only suitors left for Guerrero and Barr. Sadly, barely two weeks after the When Worlds Collide show, Barr was found dead at his home in Portland, Oregon, after having suffered a suspected heart attack.

In spite of Barr's death, a move to ECW did materialise for Guerrero - although his time with the Philadelphia promotion was fleeting at best. Still, Eddie accomplished a lot in his brief spell there, defeating Too Cold Scorpio for the ECW Television Title on his first night in in April 1995, before defending the belt in a series of matches against Dean Malenko. Guerrero would drop the title back to Too Cold Scorpio just four months later, as he moved from Philadelphia to Atlanta. Despite his short run, he had attracted the attentions of World Championship Wrestling.

Although Eddie left for WCW, he didn't make his television debut immediately, leading some to think that he would be coming in as a character. During his time in Mexico, Eddie had made several appearances for New Japan Pro Wrestling, as the masked Black Tiger character. As the second iteration of the character (following English grappler Mark "Rollerball" Rocco), Guerrero achieved some fame in the Orient against the likes of Dean Malenko and Chris Benoit - names whom would closely follow Guerrero throughout his career. Sadly, Black Tiger didn't make his way to WCW, as Guerrero finally made his debut in March 1996 under his real name, and without much of a character to speak of, save for a pretty stereotypical mustachioed Latino persona.

His WCW tenure started with some challenges for the company's United States title, losing to Konnan at the Uncensored pay-per-view in March 1996, before being beaten by Ric Flair in another title match at August's Hog Wild event. A feud with Diamond Dallas Page (DDP) followed, originally over DDP's nickname of "Lord of the Ring" - but it was this feud that eventually led Guerrero to the United State championship, as he ended the year at December's Starrcade pay-per-view beating DDP in the tournament finals to claim the belt that had been vacated following an injury to Ric Flair.

Entering 1997 as the US champion, Guerrero would go on to defend the belt in high profile matches against Scott Norton, Syxx (Sean Waltman, best known as "X-Pac" in the WWE), and Chris Jericho, before dropping the belt to Dean Malenko at the Uncensored pay-per-view. Following that defeat, Guerrero changed tack and focussed on WCW's specialised cruiserweight division, beating Jericho for the title, before embarking on a career highlight feud with Rey Mysterio. Their match at WCW's Halloween Havoc was highly rated by fans and wrestling historians, and although Guerrero lost in the title vs. mask match, Eddie would regain the belt a few weeks later. Eddie wouldn't end 1997 as WCW's Cruiserweight champion though, dropping the belt to Ultimo Dragon on the year's final edition of WCW's flagship television programme, Monday Nitro.

Having started his career wrestling against his nephew Chavo, Eddie's next step in WCW would be another family affair, as he spent several months bullying Chavo in an ongoing storyline. In a bid to "teach him a lesson", Eddie forced Chavo to act as his own personal slave. This weird relationship morphed from partnership to rivalry, with the Guerreros gunning for Ultimo Dragon's Cruiserweight title, before ending the summer of 1998 in a feud that resulted in a hair vs. hair match - a bout that Chavo would lose, before willingly shaving his head in front of his baffled uncle. After taking the hollow victory, Guerrero would depart WCW for a few months - with word going around that Eddie had thrown a cup of coffee at WCW boss Eric Bischoff in a row over a push and a pay rise (a story that was later confirmed as fabrication) - Guerrero took time off before the "hot coffee" story was weaved into a storyline... a storyline that would culminate in the formation of the Latino World Order.

Unfortunately, this being 1998, WCW was in a period where all they could do was create spin-offs of the popular New World Order (nWo) faction. Despite starting as a group of three - Hulk Hogan, Scott Hall and Kevin Nash - the nWo storyline resulted in the creation of similar groups such as nWo Hollywood (Hulk Hogan's splinter group of the nWo), nWo Wolfpack (Scott Hall and Kevin Nash's group), the One Warrior Nation (oWn - the Ultimate Warrior's spoof), the nWo Elite, the nWo Black and White (aka the "B-team" made up of non-main event wrestlers), nWo 2000, nWo Japan, and... the L... W... O.

Yes, Eddie Guerrero wound up in charge of a group of largely forgotten Latino wrestlers - a role that he was handed after WCW moved Konnan (the originally planned leader) into another arm of the nWo. The LWO would have a version of the nWo logo, in the Mexican red, white and green colours, although aside from Eddie, Rey Mysterio, Juventud Guerrera and Psychosis, the LWO wasn't much of a threat, with La Parka, Silver King, Villano V, Hector Garza, Cicolpe and El Dandy also in their ranks (but as Bret Hart quipped, who are you to doubt El Dandy?)

As the world celebrated the start of 1999, Eddie would spend New Year's Day in hospital, after being involved in a serious car accident which saw him flung through the sunroof as the car was totalled. Much like the car accident that involved Brian Pillman in April 1996, Guerrero wasn't wearing a seatbelt; but that ended up saving his life, as he would likely have suffered even worse injuries had he been strapped into the car. In spite of that, the injuries acquired would have ended most wrestlers' careers - a broken pelvis, a punctured lung, in addition to numerous cuts and bruises. Somewhat miraculously, given the injuries he sustained, Eddie was back on television, barely seven months later, returning to Monday Nitro in a match against his former LWO stable mate, Juventud Guerrera. With Eddie still not truly 100% after his remarkably-quick comeback, he was thrust into another stable, alongside Konnan and a now-unmasked Rey Mysterio: the Filthy Animals.

It was around this time that Vince Russo and Ed Ferrera jumped from the World Wrestling Federation to WCW as head writers - and with the pair charged with the task of reviving WCW's flagging fortunes, Guerrero's position in the company remained somewhat unchanged, despite the Animals being booked by Russo and Ferrera to supposedly be WCW's facsimile of WWE's D-Generation X stable.

A brief feud between the Filthy Animals and a rival faction known as the Dead Pool - Vampiro and hip-hop act the Insane Clown Posse - lasted for a few months, before they moved onto a storyline with another group: the Revolution. This would be Eddie's final storyline in WCW before taking part in a revolution of his own. Following a loss in a six-person elimination match at WCW's Mayhem pay-per-view in November 1999 - where the Animals' team of Guerrero, Billy Kidman and Torrie Wilson were beaten by the Revolution's Perry Saturn, Dean Malenko and Asya (WCW's rip-off of Chyna, get it?), Guerrero was slowly phased out of the storyline as the first incarnation of the Filthy Animals were disbanded.

Eddie Guerrero missed the Starrcade and Souled Out pay-per-views, as his character was put on the back burner whilst WCW entered a new millennium. At the same time, the winds of change started to blow through the company. The writing duo of Russo and Ferrera weren't producing the instant results that was expected of them, with WCW still a distant second behind the WWE in terms of television ratings. Even worse, WCW was shedding fans, as a result of inane storylines and endless (blank) on a pole matches; something which was a staple of Vince Russo's booking formula.

Everything came to a head in January 2000, just days before the Souled Out pay-per-view, when WCW were forced to change the card after losing Bret Hart and Jeff Jarrett to injuries (Hart was forced to retire due to concussions, and would not wrestle again for over ten years; Jarrett also missed the show due to a concussion, but he was able to return to action). With Sid Vicious needing a new challenger, various names were thrown around as to who would face - and ultimately beat - the self-named "Millennium Man". With Vince Russo suggesting Tank Abbott - a former UFC fighter who was at the time barely on the company's radar - Russo was removed from power and replaced by former wrestler Kevin Sullivan.

It was this change of power that prompted Guerrero, and several other WCW wrestlers, including Shane Douglas, Dean Malenko, Chris Benoit, Perry Saturn and Konnan, to ask for their immediate release, feeling that Sullivan would do nothing for their careers. To try and placate the unhappy wrestlers, Sullivan booked Benoit to win the WCW title from Sid Vicious - supposedly to show that he would be taking that group of performers seriously. The move didn't work, and when push came to shove, Guerrero - along with Benoit, Saturn and Malenko - asked for, and received their releases from WCW. Barely two weeks later, the four-some had a new home.

Debuting on Monday Night Raw on January 31, Guerrero appeared alongside his friends, with the group being labelled the "Radicalz". They appeared at the start of the show, sitting in the front row, with commentator Jim Ross repeatedly labelling the quartet as free agents. Before too long, the Radicalz got in on the action, jumping the rail and beating down on the New Age Outlaws, before they hit the ring, laying out the "Road Dogg" with a Dean

Malenko suplex and a Chris Benoit swandive headbutt.

In the very next segment, it was revealed that they had arrived in the WWE on the request of Mick Foley, rather than as contracted wrestlers. Indeed, the Radicalz got their chance to earn contracts on the same week's episode of SmackDown, as Triple H - and his DX - supposedly in charge of the company ordering a best of three-series, with the Radicalz earning contracts if they won the series. Dean Malenko would take on X-Pac, Chris Benoit would face Triple H, whilst the team of Eddie Guerrero and Perry Saturn would face the New Age Outlaws. DX would win all three matches, but Guerrero would dislocate his elbow whilst performing his trademark frog splash during his match, ruling him out of storylines for several weeks. As Guerrero recovered, the Radicalz turned on Mick Foley to "earn" contracts - upon his return, he would be repackaged as a new character. Thankfully, not with a new name, Eddie's character would be that of an over-the-top Latin lothario. Eddie would become "Latino Heat".

Although the Radicalz were now disbanded, the Latino Heat character would provide a springboard for Eddie's first major push in the WWE, and probably his first true push in a major promotion in North America. Unfortunately, in some people's eyes, this also meant that Eddie had to form an on-screen relationship with Chyna - an overtly muscular female wrestler (later Playboy model, then porn star) who preferred wrestling against men as opposed to women. Referring to Chyna as his "mamacita", the relationship was the first time that Guerrero was able to show any sort of character, and gave him another feather in his proverbial cap. A brief run with the WWE's European title, beating Chris Jericho for the belt, before dropping it to former Radicalz stable-mate Perry Saturn, was followed up with a rather unique role in Chyna's more conventional Intercontinental title run.

Chyna had previously held the Intercontinental championship as a "co-champion", after a double-pinfall finish in a match when she challenged then-champion Jericho. This time around, Chyna won the title in an intergender tag team match, with Guerrero and Chyna beating Trish Stratus and Val Venis in a match where the Intercontinental title was on the line. That run only lasted two weeks though, before dropping it to Guerrero in a three-way match with Kurt Angle, with the finish seeing Chyna "knocked out" when Angle hit her with the title belt, before Eddie "accidentally pinned" his on-screen girlfriend whilst trying to revive her, in order to win the belt.

After winning the Intercontinental title, the on-screen relationship between Guerrero and Chyna quickly became strained - Chyna upset at Eddie's underhanded tactics, whilst Guerrero was himself visibly upset (in storyline, at least!) to the news that Chyna was to appear in an issue of Playboy magazine. To try and keep his girlfriend sweet, Eddie proposed to Chyna - who said yes - but the engagement was called off after "hidden camera" footage caught out Eddie cavorting in the shower with two "Hos" (prostitutes bought from the WWE's resident wrestling pimp, the Godfather).

Turning heel as a result of this, the Radicalz were quickly reunited and began feuding with another reformed group - DX. Unlike the group's initial storyline in WWE, the Radicalz got the upper hand over DX, before the group splintered off again to concentrate on singles titles, with Eddie winning the European championship once again, beating Test at WrestleMania X-Seven in Houston, Texas (yes, that was WWE's way of writing WrestleMania 17 - a mish-mash of Roman and traditional numerals!). Eddie held the title for a matter of weeks, before dropping it to Matt Hardy - someone he would later align himself with, but all storylines involving Guerrero ended up being put on ice as external forces took their toll.

Still feeling the effects of the car accident on New Year's Day in 1999, Eddie had found himself addicted to painkillers, and after Dean Malenko spoke out about his concern, WWE chose to send Guerrero to rehab. After completing the course, WWE didn't rush to bring Guerrero back to television, perhaps learning the lessons that WCW hadn't in that time - somewhat coincidentally, before his departure for rehabilitation, WWE had purchased WCW - and by the end of the year, his former employer had been killed off for good after "invading" the WWE.

Whilst waiting to be called back to television, Eddie was sent to the Heartland Wrestling Association in Cincinnati - a company used by WWE in a farm league-style to develop young wrestlers. He later appeared on WWE's internet show, "Byte This", and was interviewed about his spell in rehab, claiming that he had beaten his addiction, and was feeling good for the first time in years. Guerrero claimed that his joints "used to ache when it was cold outside but not anymore. I'm not even wrestling with a brace anymore like I used to." Sadly, as Guerrero's public appearances made him look good, it quickly turned out to be a facade, and in early November, things took a turn for the worse.

An arrest for driving under the influence of alcohol isn't good news for anyone, least of all someone who had just completed a drug rehabilitation course. On November 9, 2001, Guerrero crashed into a gate at an apartment complex in Tampa, Florida. Police officers on the scene noticed that Guerrero smelled of alcohol, before promptly giving him two breath tests - both of which were failed. Days later, everything came to a head when Guerrero was given his WWE release.

The wrestling world that was waiting for Eddie after his release was a lot different to that of even a year previously. In 2001 alone, both of Guerrero's prior US employers, WCW and ECW, had closed down, with WWE taking on the best of the wrestlers from both of those promotions. Without either of those groups, Eddie's wrestling future seemed, at best, rather bleak, with local, no-name independent companies who would be only too happy to pay to have a former WWE superstar on their show seemingly being the only possible employment opportunities out there. Rather than dive into a risk-filled world of unscrupulous promoters, Eddie bided his time, and in February 2002, he jumped into bed with three promotions that were just breaking into the scene, all of whom would themselves end up with rather differing fortunes.

In the UK, Eddie accepted a booking on a show called "Revival" - an attempt to push British wrestling back into the mainstream, thanks to regular promotion on a national radio station and a leading cable and satellite TV channel in the country. Backed by former children's television presenter Tommy Boyd (who was, at the time, hosting a call-in show about wrestling on talkSPORT radio in the UK), Guerrero was included in a tournament to crown a "King of England". Although he went out in the semi-finals, to eventual tournament runner-up Doug Williams, Eddie's performance and behaviour that weekend earned him rave reviews from fans and those who worked with him.

Later that month, he went on to appear on the debut show for the Ring of Honor (ROH) promotion, wrestling former ECW alumnus Super Crazy in a match to determine the first Intercontinental champion for the Puerto Rico-based promotion, IWA. Guerrero would lose, before hopping on a plane to Las Vegas to wrestle for another new promotion, the World Wrestling All-stars (WWA). WWA was a company formed using former WCW wrestlers who were largely unable to get work with the WWE for whatever reason, with their first pay-per-view and subsequent tours of Australia and the UK featuring names like Jeff Jarrett, Gangrel, Norman Smiley and Bret Hart (acting as a commissioner for the company).

Guerrero appeared on WWA's second pay-per-view, called "The Revolution", where he would beat former LWO partners Psychosis and Juventud Guerrera to win the WWA's International Cruiserweight Championship.

By the time WWA held their next pay-per-view, "The Eruption" in April, Eddie had vacated the title - and for good reason. Ring of Honor would enjoy longevity as the number three promotion in the US, whilst WWA eventually went out of business (and the UK promotion behind Revival lasted for just one show!). Eddie was going back "home"... WWE wanted more Latino Heat.

After re-signing with WWE, Eddie made a shock return on the April Fool's Day edition of Monday Night Raw, attacking then-Intercontinental champion Rob Van Dam, initiating a major storyline for the returning Guerrero. Barely three weeks later,

Guerrero beat RVD for the title at the Backlash pay-per-view, in a move that was somewhat symptomatic of the high-speeds that WWE was starting to burn through their storylines. Guerrero would go on to defend the title successfully against Van Dam at the UK-only Insurrextion pay-per-view, and at the Judgment Day show, before losing it back to Van Dam in a ladder match on Raw. The end of that storyline was supposed to have set up Guerrero for a run with the biggest name in the business... before it went horribly wrong.

The storyline with "Stone Cold" Steve Austin started out fairly well, with Guerrero being involved in a slightly controversial segment which saw the now-sober Guerrero checking out bars whilst hunting for Austin. Unfortunately, Austin walked out on the WWE before the storyline could really get going, which forced the writers to change their plans and once again reunite Guerrero with Chris Benoit (who himself had only just returned to the company following surgery to repair a serious neck injury). That tag team with Benoit, although resulting in a brief feud against Ric Flair and a WWE title shot against the Rock, didn't really do much to push Guerrero out of the mid-card. So, to avoid him falling back into the same role of forgotten mid-card wrestler that he had long endured whilst with WCW, Guerrero was partnered with someone whom he'd had a long-standing association with: his nephew, Chavo.

Unlike their run in WCW, where the pair played off of a slavery-based storyline, this time the Guerreros were united as a pair, who lived their catchphrase of "Lie, Cheat and Steal". A series of vignettes were filmed, and broadcast on WWE's SmackDown show to promote the new team. If anyone thought that the stereotype of being sneaky Mexicans was going to get the fans to boo the Guerreros, they would have been proven wrong when the pair received cheers upon their debut.

Los Guerreros were inserted into a tournament to claim SmackDown's first set of tag team champions - at a time when WWE were treating Raw and SmackDown as separate shows with their own tag team and second-level champions. After beating Rikishi and Mark Henry in the first round, the Guerreros lost in the semi-finals to the team of Kurt Angle and Chris Benoit - the eventual winners - despite the Guerreros locking Benoit in a locker room backstage prior to their match. Despite being on the periphery of the tag team title scene, Los Guerreros would have to wait until that year's Survivor Series, when they won a three-way tag team match for the belts, with then-champions Edge and Rey Mysterio and former champs Angle and Benoit.

With the established singles wrestlers from that match heading off into their own feuds, the Guerreros found a new challenge in the form of Shelton Benjamin and Charlie Haas - Kurt Angle's lackeys as "Team Angle", later to become the "World's Greatest

Tag Team". After dropping the title to Team Angle at WrestleMania 19, Eddie was forced to find a new partner when Chavo tore his bicep in a non-televised match against independent wrestler J.R. Ryder. To make matters worse, Eddie and his new partner would have to try and regain the titles in a ladder match... so who would Eddie get as a replacement for his nephew? Step forward another former ECW alumnus: Tajiri.

The team of "Latino Heat" and the "Japanese Buzz-saw" didn't last too long, despite their tag title success in their first match together, the make-shift tandem lost the belts back to Haas and Benjamin in July 2003; a defeat that became a turning point as Eddie was transformed from a tag team specialist to a bona fide superstar in his own right.

Okay, so perhaps throwing Tajiri through the glass windshield of a low-rider wasn't the best way to turn heel when you're giving the excuse that you did it because your opponent "hit your car". This wasn't the reason why the crowd was reluctant to boo Guerrero, whose "lie, cheat and steal" character was more suited to a babyface with heel tendencies, as opposed to a full-blown heel. However, Eddie's turn on Tajiri paved the way for him to take part in a tournament to crown the first WWE United States champion - a title that was being revived, barely two years after its WCW counterpart was retired following the wrapping-up of the WCW Invasion storyline back in 2001.

After defeating Ultimo Dragon (who'd joined WWE for a brief run for a little over a year starting in the spring of 2003) and Billy Gunn, Guerrero had qualified for the tournament final against his former Radical, Chris Benoit. The final would take place at that year's Vengeance pay-per-view, and would see Guerrero win the title, capitalising on Rhyno's spear on Benoit - a move that split up that team - before claiming the pinfall victory. Shortly after retaining the title in a four-way match at SummerSlam, beating Benoit, Rhyno and Tajiri, Guerrero entered a feud with a relative newcomer in John Cena. The highlight of that particular feud was an intense "Parking Lot Brawl" for Guerrero's United States title, a match fought in amongst a variety of parked cars, which saw both combatants take bumps into cars. Guerrero retained the title thanks to the help of the returning Chavo Guerrero - a return that led to a brief reunion of Los Guerreros... and would pave the way for greater glories for Eddie.

Whilst Los Guerreros had another run with the WWE tag team titles, beating the World's Greatest Tag Team and dropping the belts to the Basham Brothers, Eddie's run as US champion lasted barely three months, dropping the belt to the Big Show, as he briefly focussed again on tag team gold. The Guerrero clan failed to recapture the tag titles, and their frustrations at missing out on the gold turned into hatred between the pair. This led Chavo to attack his uncle, prompting a match at 2004's Royal Rumble - a match that Eddie would decisively win.

Although he did not take part in the Rumble match itself, Guerrero found himself inserted into a SmackDown-only Rumble that was held days after the pay-per-view, with the winner getting a WWE title shot (the winner of the pay-per-view version, Chris Benoit, jumped from SmackDown to Raw to challenge for Triple H's World Heavyweight Championship). Guerrero, replacing Benoit from the list of SmackDown wrestlers in the initial Rumble, eventually won, and got his title shot against Brock Lesnar at the No Way Out pay-per-view at California's famed Cow Palace arena. This match would become the pinnacle of Eddie's career.

With his family watching from the front row, Guerrero went into the match against the future UFC champion Lesnar as quite the underdog. However, Lesnar could not quite overcome Guerrero, and after the referee was knocked to the mat, Lesnar went to grab his WWE title belt, so that he could strike Eddie with it and get one step closer to victory. Earlier in the night, Bill Goldberg - the former WCW champion who was coming towards the end of his first (and only) year in WWE - had appeared at the show, before being escorted out of the arena by police after getting into a confrontation and attacking Lesnar. Goldberg would return to the show, running in and hitting the Spear on Lesnar, allowing Eddie Guerrero to ultimately land his frog splash finisher for the pinfall to win the WWE title.

What happened next probably wasn't the best idea, especially for the working security guards, as Guerrero dove into the crowd and celebrated with his newly-won title and a flag of Mexico. The following week's SmackDown was the scene for a massive celebration as Eddie paraded his newly-won championship, but as things turned out, becoming WWE champion would not be a form of redemption, but rather a whole new way to crank up the pressure on Guerrero. His first major title defence would come at WrestleMania 20, where a victory over Kurt Angle paved the way for a triumphant end-of-show scene with Guerrero and his long-time Chris Benoit embraced, with the pair holding their respective WWE title belts.

After WrestleMania, Kurt Angle was forced to take time off to deal with a neck injury, which opened the door for a rather unfamiliar challenger. Enter John "Bradshaw" Layfield. Formerly known as Bradshaw, "JBL" was repackaged as a singles wrestler after his long-time tag team partner Faarooq was "fired" the week after WrestleMania. Having been known as a tag team wrestler for years, seeing JBL as a credible contender for any title was quite the stretch. Taking him serious as a threat to the WWE seemed to be impossible.

To Guerrero's credit, the feud with the former Bradshaw accomplished the impossible. With a mixture of hard-hitting matches and teetering-on-the-edge-of-being-blatantly-racist promos, Guerrero not only established JBL as a threat, but ended up putting him to the level of someone whom he would need to overcome the odds to beat, hence Guerrero "needing" to hit JBL with a low blow to escape with a disqualification loss at the Judgment Day pay-per-view. The rematch at the Great American Bash event saw Guerrero screwed out of the title in a Texas Bullrope match. With the winner being the first person to touch all four turnbuckles in a row (without being cut-off), the match headed to a dramatic finale with both men tied on three apiece. In a desperate bid to grab the victory, Eddie grabbed the rope and attempted to leapfrog over JBL en route to the final turnbuckle pad... in the process, pushing the challenger's back into the corner. Eddie's celebrations were short-lived, as Kurt Angle - by now playing the role of a heel General Manager for SmackDown - came out and stated that JBL's back had touched the turnbuckle first, and as a result, the New York loudmouth was ruled to be the winner and new WWE Champion.

Eddie's brief attempts to regain the title ended when he lost a cage match to JBL on SmackDown, thanks to the interference of a masked generic wrestler known as "El Gran Luchadore". Confusingly, Eddie had publicly assumed that character a week before on SmackDown, so when "El Gran Luchadore" came out and subdued Guerrero enough for JBL to take the victory, everyone was wondering just who the mystery Mexican was. After the match, "El Gran Luchadore" was unmasked as Kurt Angle - now healed up - setting up a storyline that would take Guerrero to the end of 2004. In truth, the move to take the title off of Guerrero had as much to do with establishing a new character as it did to ease some pressure. Behind the scenes, Guerrero was convincing himself that he wasn't worthy of being champion, and all of this self-inflicted pressure led those in charge to take the decision to take Eddie out of the firing line whilst still keeping him in a high profile storyline.

Having lost the initial match to Kurt Angle at SummerSlam, Guerrero gained a tag team partner - The Big Show - in an ongoing war with Angle, who had been joined by his two latest associates in the form of Luther Reigns and Mark Jindrak. That storyline ended up splintering out, resulting in Big Show being "harpooned" and getting his head shaved - a look he sports to this very day. But for Guerrero, the storyline did little, and it wasn't until the start of 2005 that Guerrero's spark returned.

Coming off the back of an unsuccessful attempt to win the WWE tag team titles with Booker T, Guerrero formed an alliance with a man who he was extremely familiar with - Rey Mysterio. The pair won the tag team titles at the No Way Out pay-per-view in 2005, beating the Basham Brothers for what would turn out to be the final championship that Eddie would win. Instead of defending the titles at WrestleMania 21, the champions instead wrestled each other in an entertaining match which Mysterio eventually won. That prompted some rather unfriendly rivalry between the champions, which quickly culminated barely three in the duo losing the titles to the debuting team of MNM (Joey Mercury and Johnny Nitro - later John Morrison - managed by Melina, hence MNM). A rematch the following week only served to confirm the split between Guerrero and Mysterio, with Eddie leaving his former partner bloodied and motionless after suplexing him onto the steel ring steps following their defeat.

Naturally, that served to turn Eddie heel once more, albeit with a more methodical character which morphed into a summer-long feud with Mysterio. The storyline included both the Guerrero and the "Mysterio" families, as Eddie held a family secret over the head of his former tag team partner. Instead of acting as Guerrero's slave - which would have echoed the Eddie & Chavo storyline from back in WCW - the pair had a match in which Eddie swore not to reveal the secret if he lost. Eddie lost the match, but just like an old-school heel should have done, he let the cat out of the bag anyway, revealing to the world that Rey's son Dominick was actually... Eddie's. Of course, in real life, none of this was true, but the storyline captivated fans, with SmackDown drawing its highest numbers in years amongst Latino fans, who compared the storyline to "telenovellas" (daytime soap operas). Although the feud ultimately ended when Eddie lost a ladder match, in which the custody of Dominick was laughably at stake, Guerrero somehow ended up being named the number one contender for the World Heavyweight Championship - a title held by Batista.

Still acting as a heel, Eddie subtly modified his character as he pretended to be Batista's friend - supposedly to save himself from a beating he would have gotten had he been Batista's full-blown enemy. Despite losing to Batista at 2005's No Mercy pay-per-view, and "respecting" the champion after the match, Eddie still continued to chase for the title. When Batista suffered a torn latissimus (back muscle) in mid November, WWE quickly chose to give the champion some time off to recover from the muscle tear, writing in a three-way match on the following week's SmackDown between Batista, Randy Orton and Eddie Guerrero as a way to change the title on Batista's way out. Sadly, Eddie never got that match.

Although Raw and SmackDown were usually held on Monday (live for Raw) and Tuesday (taped for SmackDown), an impending tour of Europe meant that WWE had decided to record both Raw and SmackDown on the same evening in Minneapolis, Minnesota. After having caught a flight to Minneapolis with his cousin Chavo, Eddie had been staying in a Marriott hotel prior to that evening's television tapings. When Eddie didn't answer his wake-up call on the morning of November 13, Chavo called security, who entered the room, only to find Eddie slumped across the bathroom sink. Despite Chavo's attempts at CPR, it was too late - another loss had been inflicted on the wrestling world.

The news was quickly broken by WWE on their website, with a candid story later providing quotes from his widow Vickie (who had been with Eddie for most of his adult life, having dated him as a youngster) stating that the autopsy had revealed that Eddie's past abuse of drink and drugs had been his downfall. Whilst Eddie had reportedly been clean for four years, the damage had already been done - the years of steroid and painkiller use, and the lingering effects of the 1999 car accident had caught up with him.

That same day, business had to be done as WWE still had television shows to produce. Much like they had done with Owen Hart in 1999, the script for Raw and SmackDown were thrown out of the window. Instead, both shows became tributes to Eddie Guerrero, in the same vein as the "Raw is Owen" show, with no wrestler being forced to work, but all invited to record their own tributes to Eddie, which would be played on Raw, SmackDown... or dumped onto WWE.com if you weren't a big enough star. Among the tributes was a virtual confirmation by Stephanie McMahon (by that point, a leading figure in WWE's creative department) that Eddie was to have won Batista's World Heavyweight title during that evening's tapings, and an angst-ridden tribute by a tearful Chris Benoit - a video that became all the more haunting following Benoit's passing less than two years later.

In the days after Eddie's death, with the wrestling world still reeling, WWE nearly had another tragedy on its hands, after Nick Dinsmore (who wrestled at the time as Eugene) was found passed out in the lobby of a hotel in Manchester, England, just days into the company's European tour. Bizarrely, given the company's history, WWE again acknowledged this on their website, and even confirmed that Dinsmore had passed out due to an overdose of the muscle relaxant carisoprodol, also known as "somas". Dinsmore was quickly flown back to the US, where he was signed up into a rehabilitation facility. On the same day, WWE would also announce another major change to their infrastructure - they would bring back drug testing.

Again, wanting to portray this to the wider world, WWE's website posted a video from backstage in the arena in Sheffield, England, where Vince McMahon announced the news to all of the wrestlers present on the tour, specifically stating that he would be given the news from the drug testers after the wrestlers had been told themselves (so there would be no case of management "forgetting" to pass the news on), and that there would be no "special exemptions". Whilst the exemptions part wasn't strictly true (the policy only applied to wrestlers on a permanent talent contract - so someone like Vince, who only made sporadic in-ring appearances, would be exempt), the news clearly made a few wrestlers nervous, with Kurt Angle in particular being shown on the video to ask about whether they'd be testing for prescription medication and how they would determine what was abuse.

WWE did post the Wellness Policy on their website, stating that the company now prohibited the use of steroids in any circumstance (both testosterone and anything based on testosterone, such as stanozolol), as well as recreational or "non-medical" usage of various street drugs (ecstasy, cocaine, morphine and their variants), diuretics, muscle relaxants and even painkillers. In short, if your usual doctor didn't prescribe it to you for a valid reason, you weren't allowed to test positive!

Whilst the main focus of the Wellness Policy concerned drug testing, the company also introduced cardiovascular tests, perhaps on the idea that if WWE had been aware of the damage that had been done to Eddie's heart, they wouldn't have promoted him as much (or indeed, given him the full time schedule that he had had). Less than two years after the testing was introduced, wrestler Montel Vontavious Porter (aka "MVP) received the diagnosis of a condition known as Wolff–Parkinson–White syndrome, a heart condition which carries the risk of sudden cardiac arrest. MVP was given time off as doctors assessed his condition, but whilst the cardiac tests may have flagged up some wrestlers who may have had their lives saved as a result, the headline story - the drugs tests - played havoc with the WWE's cards. Days before a pay-per-view in July 2006, the Great American Bash, test results came in that forced Bobby Lashley and the Great Khali to be pulled from the card. At around the same time, seven more performers were also suspended as a result of the company's new Wellness Policy, with the likes of Rob Van Dam (suspended after being caught with marijuana by police) and Kurt Angle (given time off to deal with a prescription pill issue that eventually led to his firing by WWE later in the summer of 2006) being snared by the new rules, prompting even more headaches on a creative team that was struggling to cope with the task of creating interesting scenarios whilst working with a crew of characters that was trying to adjust to the business' new landscape.

Away from the impact that the Wellness Policy created, the Guerrero family had to adjust to life without their figurehead. A widower, Vickie found her way into the business that she had seen her husband devote his entire life to. Although she had had some cameo appearances in the 2005 "Dominik is Eddie's son" storyline with her husband and Rey Mysterio, Vickie became something of an on-screen character as Mysterio successfully mounted a challenge for the World Heavyweight Championship. Her role as a motivator slowly segued into that of a hated figure, after turning her back on Mysterio after attacking him with a steel chair and sided with her nephew-in-law Chavo Guerrero.

Since then, Vickie has been used in various roles as a perennial heel character, including storyline relationships with Edge (whom she married on TV), Eric Escobar (a Puerto Rican wrestler whose WWE career was over in the blink of an eye) and Dolph Ziggler. Away from love interests, Vickie has also been portrayed as someone of an authority figure, having fulfilled the role of General Manager of SmackDown and Raw on several occasions, whilst also (bizarrely) being a "Pro" on the all-female season of WWE's NXT show, where Vicki saw her "rookie" replaced just days before the show started - her initial rookie, Aloisia, was fired by WWE following revelations from her past, and was replaced with the season's eventual winner, Kaitlyn.

CHRIS BENOIT

(May 21, 1967 - June 24, 2007)

Unlike Owen Hart or Eddie Guerrero, Chris Benoit started life as a wrestling fan in Edmonton, often going to one of Stu Hart's Stampede Wrestling shows, where he would idolise the Dynamite Kid. Meeting his idol backstage at a Stampede show in his home town, only made Benoit more determined to become a professional wrestler.

Thanks to a set of weights purchased by his father, Benoit put in the time in the gym and turned from a scrawny kid who sat in the crowd, to a more defined man who was about to take his first steps into professional wrestling. He travelled to Calgary to be trained by Stu Hart in the world-famous Dungeon. Benoit eventually made his in-ring debut on November 22, 1985 for Stampede Wrestling in a tag team match, where he was billed as "Dynamite" Chris Benoit - a homage to his childhood idol.

Benoit largely stayed on the local scene, and wrestled in Stampede up until it's closing in 1989 - by which point he made the move to Japan, training in the New Japan dojo. Despite having wrestled under his real name in Japan in 1986, Benoit was given a new character: the Pegasus Kid. Although in hindsight, such a character didn't seem to mesh with

Benoit, the Pegasus Kid really fit in amongst a Japanese wrestling scene that contained wrestlers such as Jushin "Thunder" Liger, Black Tiger and El Samurai - characters that looked to come straight out of the pages of comic books, whilst still being serious workers in the ring.

Through word of mouth, and the trading of tapes of his matches in Japan, Benoit slowly started to carve out a name for himself, with a series of matches against Jushin "Thunder" Liger producing memorable results. In November 1991, one of these matches saw Benoit lose his Pegasus Kid mask and character after suffering a defeat to Liger - a loss that saw Benoit reinvent his character into the Wild Pegasus. It was under this new moniker that Benoit would win the 1994 Super J Cup Tournament - but in the time since becoming Wild, he would have his first flirtation with the North American wrestling scene, courtesy of some blink-and-you'll-miss-them appearances in WCW, including a NWA tag team tournament loss with his best friend Biff Wellington (Shayne Bower).

By the end of 1994, however, Benoit was becoming a regular in an upstart promotion based out of Philadelphia: Extreme Championship Wrestling. Having worked for ECW in-between tours of Japan, Benoit was given a huge push in the company, and accidentally gained the character of the "Crippler", thanks in part to a match with Sabu in November 1994. That match ended prematurely, when Sabu botched a face-first pancake bump, instead under-rotating for what should have been a back bodydrop. This confusion resulting in Sabu landing on his head, causing him to break his neck. Sabu would eventually wrestle again, and sustain plenty more injuries in his career (including countless cuts that were glued back together, and a broken jaw that he wrestled through after wrapping his mouth together in duct tape!)

Privately, Benoit was freaking out that he may have paralysed and ended the career of a fellow professional wrestler. However, ECW booker Paul Heyman instead opted to use this incident to emphasise Benoit's "cold blooded" character and ensure that the nickname of "The Crippler" stuck with him for the majority of his career. Despite having held the ECW tag team titles, and being in line for a run with the ECW heavyweight title, that promotion's notorious lack of back-office organisation resulted in Benoit's work visa expiring, forcing the Canadian to return to New Japan until the required paperwork was completed. In the meantime, New Japan had struck up a talent exchange deal with WCW, which gave Benoit a back door return to WCW just as that company was preparing to embark on its biggest run ever.

Although he spent most of his first year back in WCW technically working under the New Japan banner, Benoit's first real crack in WCW was as a part of one of that company's iconic stables - the Four Horsemen. Throughout WCW's run, the Horsemen had undergone numerous changes since its inception as the quartet of Ric Flair, Arn Anderson, Ole Anderson and Tully Blanchard. The 1995 flavour still kept Ric and Arn, but added Brian Pillman and Chris Benoit to the group, as Ric Flair's feud with new arrivals from the WWE such as Hulk Hogan and Randy Savage expanded to something resembling gang warfare.

Whilst the Horsemen would remain as a group, the two new arrivals would splinter off into their own storylines, starting with Pillman's bizarre feud with Kevin Sullivan - a feud that was designed to showcase Pillman's unpredictable "loose cannon" persona. Pillman somehow managed to one-up them by convincing them to give him his release from the company, in order to develop his new persona in the decidedly less-family-friendly ECW. Unfortunately for WCW, their plan to bring him back to the company backfired, when he chose to sign for the WWE in the midst of their ongoing "Monday Night Wars". With Pillman gone, Benoit was substituted into the Sullivan feud - a move that would have effects for all involved both on- and off-screen.

By this point, the Four Horsemen had numerous female valets, including Woman (Nancy Sullivan) - who in real life was married to Kevin Sullivan. As WCW hadn't quite learned from Brian Pillman burning their proverbial fingers in their last flirtation with realistic storylines, Sullivan - who was the man in charge of WCW's storylines at the time - insisted that the storyline between himself and Benoit should be as believable as possible. For reasons which were never really understood, Sullivan wrote a storyline that saw Woman become Benoit's on-screen love interest, whilst ensuring that their on-screen chemistry was as real as possible by coercing the pair to stay in the same hotel rooms whilst travelling and appearing in public together.

In a move that was not entirely unexpected, the relationship between Chris and Nancy became a full-blown love affair that ultimately led to Nancy divorcing Kevin and marrying Chris. During this period, the storyline between Benoit and Sullivan gained an edge, with WCW television airing a video of Chris in Kevin and Nancy's home, taking a shot at his rival by saying "you consider yourself the master of human chess. Well, my bishop just took your queen." Woman was removed from television in May 1997, before the fake/real rivalry came to a head when Benoit beat Sullivan in July 1997's Bash at the Beach pay-per-view in a Retirement match. This would prove to be Sullivan's final match before taking a full-time behind the scenes role in WCW.

Benoit's next big assignment would be a lengthy series of matches with Booker T, as the pair initially locked horns over the WCW Television title. After trading the title back and forth on live events (which really didn't make sense, given the Television title was only meant to be defended on TV!), Fit Finlay ended up winning the title from Booker, meaning that the ongoing feud between Booker and Benoit became a Best-of-Seven series to get a shot at what was WCW's third-tier title. After taking a 3-1 lead in the series, Benoit would conspire to throw away the lead and force a seventh and deciding match, which Benoit looked to have won, thanks to interference from Bret "Hitman" Hart. Refusing to take the win in that fashion, Benoit admitted that he'd won with some extra help - a move that saw Booker awarded a disqualification victory, only for Booker too to reject the win, forcing the deciding match to be replayed at the Great American Bash in 1998. Benoit lost the second decider, going down to a missile dropkick as Booker went on to win the Television title from Finlay later on in the same pay-per-view event. Although he left the feud without the gold, this series of matches propelled Benoit's single career into a solid mid-card position, but it wasn't until he turned to the tag team division that WCW gold returned to the waist of the "Crippler".

A reformation of the Four Horsemen coincided with Benoit teaming with former ECW alumni Dean Malenko, with the pair unseating the West Texas Rednecks - Curt Hennig and Barry Windham - leading to an ongoing feud against the likes of Billy Kidman and Rey Mysterio, or Raven and Perry Saturn. However, the Horsemen reunion didn't last long, as Benoit splintered away from the group with Malenko, eventually forming a new group known as the "Revolution".

The Revolution were created at a time when WCW was hoping to use more reality-based storylines to connect with the audience, as the company started to flounder behind a resurgent WWE. Starring Benoit alongside Dean Malenko, Perry Saturn and Shane Douglas, the group were bound together by their privately-held hatred of WCW's backstage politics. Only problem was, it was only the hardcore, internet-savvy fans of WCW who were aware of this - the vast majority of their fans weren't online, and as such, the whole Revolution storyline just did not resonate with them. During the Revolution's existence, WCW fell into the booking hands of Vince Russo, who became a false messiah as their hopes of a revival fell by the wayside.

It was during this run that Benoit had two of his more heartfelt moments in wrestling - firstly, at a house show in Baltimore, Maryland in September, paying tribute to WCW referee Mark Curtis (Brian Hildebrand). Benoit, along with his Revolution team mates, spoke candidly about Curtis, just days after he had passed away days following a fight with cancer. A rather more public memorial came in October 1999, when Benoit wrestled Bret Hart on an episode of Nitro in Kansas City - held in the same arena where Bret's brother Owen had passed away in May of that year. In a great technical match, that jarred somewhat given WCW's product at the time, Benoit refused to go over Bret, insisting that "the Hitman" won the match in tribute to Owen.

As 1999 became 2000, Benoit's time in WCW was numbered, as he left the company alongside Eddie Guerrero and close friends Dean Malenko and Perry Saturn. Whilst Guerrero, Saturn and Malenko had been underused, Benoit's departure caught WCW off guard, as they had made him the company's champion. Truth be told, the move - which came after Vince Russo was fired for having the brain-wave of making Tank Abbott champion - was a last ditch ploy to keep Benoit and co. happy. With Kevin Sullivan back in charge of WCW, Benoit knew that bygones wouldn't remain bygones, and his longevity as a top line wrestler in WCW would remain extremely limited. Surprisingly, Benoit was allowed to leave WCW, despite being champion - although a lot of that was down to alleged threats of violence made towards Benoit by then-WCW road agent Mike Graham - allegations that made it a lot more straightforward to just let him go than hold him to his contract.

In the WWE, Benoit debuted on Raw as part of the Radicalz - alongside Eddie Guerrero et al (which is why I'm not repeating the Radicalz's early days). Whilst the rest of the Radicalz quickly settled into the midcard though, Benoit was given somewhat of a push towards the WWE's main events, having won the Intercontinental championship at WrestleMania 2000 in a two-of-three-falls match for Kurt Angle's two titles (Chris Jericho won the European title in the second fall, leaving Angle belt-less by the end of the show). After dropping the title to Rikishi in June, Benoit found himself in the picture for the WWE title -

initially losing to the Rock at the Fully Loaded pay-per-view in July 2000 (despite "winning", the match was restarted due to outside interference, which led to Benoit ultimately losing). That match was followed up with Benoit appearing in a four-way for the title at Unforgiven two months later, but with a similar fate, losing to the Rock Bottom.

Away from the WWE title, Benoit crossed paths numerous times with Chris Jericho, culminating in an entertaining ladder match at the 2001 Royal Rumble that saw Jericho lift the title. Benoit remained in storylines though, losing to Kurt Angle at WrestleMania 17 - a show that was somewhat overshadowed by the WWE's purchase of WCW. Shortly after WrestleMania, Benoit started to team up with Jericho, with the duo winning the tag team titles from Steve Austin and Triple H in a match that was marred by Triple H suffering a serious quadriceps tear as he tried to break up a Walls of Jericho submission. Just 24 hours later, Benoit and Jericho defended their titles in a four-way Tables, Ladders and Chairs (TLC) match against Edge & Christian, the Hardy Boyz and the Dudleyz. In a sign of the times, the TLC match received little advance promotion, and resulted in a serious injury, with Benoit suffering a broken neck from a rather innocuous move: a missed big splash off the top of a ladder, as Benoit crashed through the table after Matt Hardy got out of the way. Benoit was stretchered out of the arena, with the initial fears being that he had broken his ribs, but in truth the injury was far more severe than anyone thought.

In spite of the injury, Benoit would continue to wrestle for almost a month afterwards as his ongoing storyline saw himself and Chris Jericho fail to unseat Steve Austin for the WWE title, both in separate one-on-one matches then in a three-way match at the 2001 King of the Ring pay-per-view. Although the three-way saw Benoit and Jericho force a submission when their holds were used in tandem, the match was restarted until a clear winner was decided.

Benoit would get surgery to repair his broken neck shortly after that match - surgery that would pin him to the sidelines for over a year. Despite being off of television, Benoit was "drafted" to SmackDown as the WWE's brand extension saw the company split into two distinct shows with their own travelling crew. Picked as SmackDown's third choice in the initial draft in March 2002, it was only natural that Benoit would return a few months later... on Raw! His spell on Monday night's was short lived - but long enough for Benoit to dethrone Rob Van Dam as the company's Intercontinental champion before being moved onto SmackDown, completely ignoring the initial draft storyline. Unfortunately, the Intercontinental title went back to Raw, after Benoit dropped the title back to Van Dam at SummerSlam 2002, but it wasn't long before gold would be around the Crippler's waist - in the form of the newly created WWE Tag Team Championships.

These tag team titles were awarded to the team of Chris Benoit and Kurt Angle following a tournament of teams of SmackDown wrestlers. Unfortunately, the tandem known to some as "God's Team" (due to their wrestling ability) would have a brief run with the titles, as they would drop the belts to the team of Edge and Rey Mysterio just weeks later. In the fall-out from that, Angle would move onto winning the WWE title, whilst Benoit ended up in feuds against the Full Blooded Italians and an up and coming John Cena. It took a feud with SmackDown General Manager Paul Heyman to start Benoit's push to the top - and almost as a metaphor for his whole career to date, he'd have to get to the top the hard way.

After winning a 2-on-3 match, teaming with John Cena to overcome the FBI, Benoit qualified for the 2004 Royal Rumble, only to be forced to be the first entrant in the match by Heyman. History would go on to show Benoit winning the match, lastly eliminating the Big Show, leaving the door open for a title shot against SmackDown's WWE champion Brock Lesnar, right? It wasn't quite that simple - Benoit jumped to Raw to challenge for Triple H's World Heavyweight Championship in a match that ended up becoming a triple-threat match, as Shawn Michaels added himself to the match. In the meantime, Benoit's "spot" on SmackDown would end up going to his close friend Eddie Guerrero, who beat Brock Lesnar for the title a month later, before defending the belt at WrestleMania 20 against Kurt Angle.

Benoit's match would end up being the main event. It was enthralling and would gain the acclaim of the fans both inside Madison Square Garden and those watching at home on pay-per-view around the world. Benoit made Triple H submit to the Crossface, securing his first World title belt. WrestleMania would end with a memorable scene, with both Benoit and Eddie Guerrero embracing each other, title belts in hand, as confetti rained down on the arena.

After successfully defending the title in a re-match at Backlash, Benoit lifted Raw's version of the tag team titles, teaming with Edge to beat Triple H's Evolution stable-mates of Ric Flair and Batista. With two titles in hand, Benoit would go on to a feud with Kane over the World Heavyweight title, whilst also having to fend off the challenge of La Resistance for the tag titles. At June's Bad Blood PPV, Benoit lost the tag titles but retained the big one - before losing to Randy Orton at SummerSlam as WWE quickly crowned a new "youngest world champion" following the departure of Brock Lesnar earlier in the year.

Shortly after dropping the title, Benoit would engage in a feud with Edge after their attempts to regain the tag titles from La Resistance failed. The pair would have matches on and off for the best part of the following year, including a Last Man Standing match which was won when Edge hit Benoit with a brick. This preceded a move back to SmackDown for Benoit, and the start of a series of "blink-and-you'll-miss-them" matches against Orlando Jordan for the United States title, which started after Jordan somehow defeated Benoit. With the internet community in uproar at seeing their hero lose to a rookie like Jordan, Benoit would quite literally squash him to lift the US title, needing just 25 seconds to win the title at 2005's SummerSlam. A series of rematches were in 23.4 and 22.5 seconds - enough time to literally make a cup of coffee, as Benoit demonstrated courtesy of a split-screen.

A brief feud with Booker T didn't exactly rekindle the memories of their best-of-seven feud from WCW, but it did lead to them trading the title back and forth as 2005 became 2006. Shortly after his first title defeat, Benoit would endure a personal hell, after Eddie Guerrero was found dead in a hotel room in Minnesota. Breaking down in grief during a video tribute to his friend, Benoit would have little choice but to piece his life back together and continue in the career that had taken the life of one of his closest friends.

With Benoit eventually ending the feud with Booker T as US champion, he would move on to a new feud. A feud with a man whose career had been revived by Benoit's closest friend - and just like Eddie Guerrero some two years earlier, Benoit would be on the losing end of a title match with John "Bradshaw" Layfield. The feud would be short lived, as Benoit moved into a brief series with Finlay, before injuries forced him to the sidelines for a few months.

Making his return at No Mercy in October 2006, as a surprise opponent for William Regal (who had inadvertently exposed himself earlier in the show; pro tip: if you're being written to wear nothing but a towel, make sure you can't accidentally bare all!), Benoit would go onto win the US title back from another newcomer - Mr Kennedy - before being thrust into what was his last major feud, against Montel Vontavious Porter (MVP). A former champion, MVP would claim to be the best US champion in history, which was the precursor for the inevitable match at WrestleMania 23, only for MVP to win the title in a 2-of-3-falls match two months later.

Well away from the World and United State title pictures, Benoit found himself drafted to the revived ECW brand in June 2006. The intention was for Benoit to be a trainer of sorts, working with the inexperienced talent on ECW, whilst also spearheading the brand, with plans for Benoit to win the brand's championship belt after it had been vacated by Bobby Lashley. A victory over Elijah Burke pushed Benoit into a tournament final against CM Punk. A title match was to have taken place at the Vengeance: Night of Champions pay-per-view on June 24. The events of that weekend overshadowed not just that one match, but a wrestler's entire career.

According to a timeline released by WWE in June 2007, Benoit missed a non-televised event in Beaumont, Texas on June 23rd - claiming that his wife, Nancy, and his son, Daniel, were vomiting blood as a result of a bout of food poisoning. With Benoit apparently having his flights rebooked to make it to the pay-per-view in Houston, Texas for the next day, all was assumed to be well, that was, until a series of unusual text messages were sent.

In the early hours of morning of the pay-per-view, text messages were sent from Chris' phone to two colleagues - Chavo Guerrero and WWE referee Scott Armstrong - giving his "physical address" as well as the worrying information "The dogs are in the enclosed pool area. Garage side door is open". At around the same time, Nancy's phone was used to text the same "physical address". Benoit did not make it to Houston, and when those text messages were received the day after the show, the police were called to the Benoit family home in Fayetteville, Georgia. What they discovered was truly harrowing.

Upon entering the property, Fayette County police discovered the bodies of Chris Benoit, his wife Nancy and 7-year-old son Daniel. WWE immediately called off that evening's live show of Monday Night Raw, opting instead to fill the three hour slot with a modified version of their now-typical tribute format, with comments from wrestlers being inserted in-between clips from the WWE's career retrospective DVD for Benoit, entitled "Hard Knocks". To make matters worse, the three-hour show had meant to have been holding a faked funeral for Vince McMahon, whose character had been killed off some weeks earlier after he climbed into a limo which then blew up. As the Chris Benoit tribute was broadcast, however, the grisly facts started to emerge, and questions slowly started to be answered.

Police investigations quickly deduced that the crime scene at the Benoit house was actually the scene of a murder/suicide. Nancy's body was found in a upstairs room, with her hands and legs tied together, and her body covered in a towel, with the police theorising that Benoit had strangled his wife to death with the use of an electrical or telephone cord. Daniel Benoit was found suffocated to death in his bedroom, with toxicology results showing that he had been given a dose of the anti-depressant drug Xanax, which would likely have left him unconscious at the time of his murder.

After murdering his wife and son, Chris Benoit then took his own life, with police finding his body hanging from a weightlifting machine. Removing a pull-down bar and fashioning the steel cable into a noose, Benoit wrapped a towel around his neck, then the wire noose, before using the weightlifting machine to hang himself.

Although no suicide was originally found - one was found inserted in a Bible that was passed onto his previous wife in amongst his personal effects - police discovered a Bible left next to the bodies of both Nancy and Daniel. In the hours that followed, WWE embarked on a mission to erase Benoit from their history books - the tribute edition of Raw was never replayed, and was instead replaced internationally with a collection of some of the WWE's best matches from recent months. All Benoit merchandise and DVDs focused on him were pulled from sale, whilst the DVDs of any pay-per-views that he was involved in saw his name and/or match removed from all advertising. Stories on the company website were edited and written to remove Benoit, with recaps of WrestleMania XX in particular now painting Eddie Guerrero vs. Kurt Angle as the show's main event, instead of what really headlined that show in Madison Square Garden.

To this day, WWE go out of their way to exclude Benoit in any video releases, either in mentioning his name, or showing his image. Although they have released some of his matches, or matches where he has a cameo, he is not promoted or featured, and at times, the footage has been edited to include him as little as possible. Understandably, it's at the point where Benoit's name is up there with the company's old WWF logo and initials in terms of "things that must not be mentioned on anything we release".

In the days and weeks that followed, a massive spotlight was shone onto the wrestling business, with news talk shows throughout North America speculating as to what could have been responsible for these murders. Was it steroids? Was it a combination of other prescription drugs? Was it caused by the results of chair shots? Was it caused by the combination of the other artefacts of his hard-hitting wrestling style? Or was it something else that we'd all experienced - death. Fans across the world were witness to Benoit's quite public breakdown on television following the passing of Eddie Guerrero, but it was only part of the puzzle, as Benoit appeared to struggle to cope with the death of many wrestlers whom he'd travelled with over the years: Johnny Grunge (formerly of ECW cult tag team "Public Enemy") was a death that hit Benoit particularly hard, coming barely three months after Guerrero's passing. Just days before Benoit took his own life, a former tag team partner from his early days in Stampede - Biff Wellington - was found dead after an apparent heart attack, although it is unlikely that Benoit was aware of this.

As all interested parties awaited the results of autopsies and toxicology reports, claims and counter-claims were thrown all over the place. Active WWE wrestlers appeared on news shows to defend their employers - some coming across in a positive manner, others not so - as former WWE employees and wrestling reporters also threw in their two cents. Then, when the tests came back, it all started to make sense.

Despite having had a Wellness Policy in place for over eighteen months by this point, the toxicology results showed that Chris Benoit had extremely elevated levels of testosterone in his body. Whilst representatives from the WWE had acknowledged

Benoit's steroid use - he had been given a "therapeutic use exemption" for steroid testing in the Wellness Policy - very few people could have defended just how elevated his testosterone levels (caused by injecting steroids) were. The tests conducted on his body registered his levels at a staggeringly high 59:1 ratio.

Whilst the levels of Xanax and hydrocodone (Vicodin) present in Benoit's body were at fairly normal levels, the absurdly high levels of testosterone just added credibility to the claims that the most important part of WWE's Wellness Policy was nothing but a sham. After all, how else could you explain having a wrestler somehow pass various drug tests (where a 10:1 ratio between testosterone and epitestosterone is a failure), yet have levels almost six times greater than what would have been classed as a test failure at the time of his death?

Other tests showed that Benoit's brain had suffered extensive damage, with the Sports Legacy Institute finding that his brain had a disease known as chronic traumatic encephalopathy (CTE). Although it can only be positively diagnosed after death, CTE is usually characterised in the living with symptoms such as memory loss, aggression, depression and confusion. At the same time as diagnosing Benoit's CTE, the Sports Legacy Institute - headed up by former WWE wrestler Christopher Nowinski - declared that the brain injuries suffered by Benoit had left him with a brain akin to that of an 85 year old Alzheimer's sufferer. That particular declaration raised eyebrows, not least amongst those who worked with him every day, noting that, at work, Benoit did not fulfil any of those criteria. After all, when was the last time you saw an 80-something-year-old wrestle, let alone someone with Alzheimer's?

The After Effects

It's no surprise that professional wrestling has to deal with death so often. After all, we're still living in a time where those who wrestled in the days of territories are still alive - and the increased number of people involved in the sport, it's only natural that the death toll is higher. Although there are a fair number of those who died of natural causes and of old age, there are also plenty of cases where wrestlers are dying before their time.

Without turning into Marc Mero and pulling out a list of every wrestler who's died who's been employed by any of WWE, WCW, ECW or TNA, a selection of the names of those who had recently been a mainstream star anywhere in the world makes for depressing reading:

1997: Brian Pillman (heart disease)
1998: Louie Spicolli (drug overdose)
1999: Owen Hart (fall), Richard Wilson (WCW's "Renegade, committed suicide), "Ravishing" Rick Rude (heart attack)
2000: Yokozuna (heart attack)
2001: Terry Gordy (heart attack), Chris Adams (shot)
2002: "The British Bulldog" Davey Boy Smith (heart failure), "Flyboy" Rocco Rock (heart attack)

2003: Curt Hennig (best known as "Mr Perfect", drug overdose), Road Warrior Hawk (heart attack), Crash Holly (suicide)

2004: Ray Traylor (best known as the "Big Bossman", heart attack)

2005: Chris Candido (blood clot/complications from surgery), Eddie Guerrero (heart attack)

2006: John Tenta (best known as "Earthquake", cancer)

2007: Mike Awesome (suicide), Bam Bam Bigelow (drug overdose), Sherri Martel (drug overdose), Brian Adams (best known as "Crush"), Chris Benoit (suicide), Nancy Benoit (best known as "Woman", murdered)

2009: Andrew "Test" Martin (drug overdose), Mitsuharu Misawa (spinal cord injury during a match), Eddie Fatu (best known as "Umaga", acute toxicity after drug overdose), Steve Williams (cancer)

2010: Chris Kanyon (suicide), Lance Cade (heart failure)

2011: "Macho Man" Randy Savage (heart disease)

Just the sheer length of this list is depressing to read. Once you take into mind that out of this list, two of the deaths actually took place during a wrestling event, four were suicides, six were attributed to drug overdoses (or the effects of drugs) and ten were heart attacks or heart failures, questions have to be asked. Even looking at just the eight-or-so years prior to Eddie Guerrero's death, the loss of wrestlers to heart attacks and drug overdoses meant that questions were being asked long before the phrase "wellness policy" became a part of WWE's lexicon.

Whilst it is true that WWE did have a drug testing policy in place in the 1990s - a policy that was abolished in the mid 90s to save money, when the company was quickly running out of cash - it is also fair to say that this policy only really was applied whilst you were with the company, especially with rival promotion WCW not having much of an effective drugs policy to speak of. In the case of the British Bulldog, although he was fired by WWE in late 1992 (reportedly for receiving shipments of Human Growth Hormone, possibly in a bid to subvert any possible steroids testing), Davey Boy Smith simply went home to England and wrestled there before being picked up by WCW, where his chemically-enhanced physique showed no changes. That seemed to be the running theme in the world of wrestling - if a company with a testing policy caught you taking drugs, you either got off them or left for a company that didn't test. In the 90s, it was WCW. In the 2000s, it was TNA. Even after the death of Eddie Guerrero, although the numbers of wrestlers dying young slowed somewhat, there still were the few wrestlers who managed to make a mockery of the tests. In August 2007, Sports Illustrated magazine revealed a list of wrestlers whom were on the list of clients of Signature Pharmacy - a company which prescribed and delivered drugs to clients, including painkillers, muscle relaxants and steroids.

Although at the time, WWE weren't revealing names of people who had failed their Wellness Policy, WWE did confirm that ten wrestlers had been suspended following the Signature Pharmacy bust. Unfortunately, subsequent news reports from the New York Times and ESPN provided the names of WWE performers past and present who had been caught out by Signature Pharmacy.

The mis-count sparked a new furore against the WWE, especially when their own Wellness Policy was supposed to prevent performers from using other doctors and online pharmacies to obtain medication. As this came at a time where WWE were still reeling from the Benoit murder-suicide, it resulted in yet more clampdowns in the company's drug-testing policy, although it seemed that, at least for the active WWE wrestlers who were on the list, if they hadn't been receiving deliveries since the company's Wellness Policy came into effect, they would avoid any suspension. Regardless, the story caused yet more headaches for the company, with top-line wrestlers such as Mr. Kennedy being busted by the Signature Pharmacy scandal as having received steroids a year after the Wellness Policy came into force - this coming just a few months after he'd volunteered to appear in front of the US news media to defend the company post-Benoit and state that he had stopped taking steroids when the policy was brought in. Whoops!

In the aftermath of those embarrassing revelations, WWE started developing their Wellness Policy further. Punishment for failing a test for marijuana was changed from a suspension to a $1,000 fine - a move that led to some wrestlers taking the synthetic alternative known as "spice" and risk getting suspended, as opposed to paying the so-called "pot tax".

Aside from the reformation of the Wellness Policy, WWE also found themselves forced onto previously unchartered territory. As the revelations regarding Benoit's brain hit the news, a new hot topic came to the fore: concussions. In days gone by, wrestlers would be used to getting concussions and wrestling on despite not having recovered from them, especially in Benoit's case, wrestling with a concussion (or several!) became something of a badge of honour. After all, if you could wash down a few painkillers to make the pain go away, and still perform and get paid handsomely, what's the problem? Well, as we are finding out now, the problem is turning out to be a rather troublesome one.

In the weeks after Benoit's death, members of the Sports Legacy Institute were all over the media with their take on the concussion issue. One member, Julian Bailes, stated that CTE could start becoming noticeable after just two concussions - a scary prospect in a wrestling industry in which concussions had been seen as that badge of honour. Since the

Benoit incident, WWE has taken many precautions against wrestlers with concussions, with wrestlers such as Randy Orton finding themselves removed from the line of fire for several weeks as they recovered from concussions (in Orton's case, he was removed from shows in June 2011 until he passed a brain function test known as an "Impact test", before he eventually returned to action).

And what of Owen Hart? His death, although put down to a tragic accident, did have some repercussions, if only for a short period of time. The use of relatively pointless stunts in wrestling, such as rappelling from the ceiling of the arena into the ring quickly vanished as wrestling sought to make themselves safe - at least until the bell rang. Whilst these stunts slowly crept back into the business, albeit on a more controlled level, with the use of stunt co-ordinators, it took the tragedies of Eddie Guerrero and Chris Benoit for the business to get serious about making the lifestyle as a whole safer. Introducing the Wellness Policy was a good starting point, but the fallout from the Benoit murder-suicide only served to underline that actions, not words were needed.

In the time since the Benoit tragedy, wrestling as a whole started to phase out the needless moves and stunts that caused the brain trauma that some said contributed to the whole scenario; mainly, the use of unprotected chair shots in wrestling. During the late 90s, when both WWE and WCW were jumping on the ECW-inspired "hardcore wrestling" bandwagon, matches regularly featured the use of weapons, with a folding steel chair regularly being aimed at the head of a combatant. Most of the time, the impact of the chair shots aimed to the head were reduced by the recipient putting their hand in the way, producing the same sound that the shot would have done had it hit the head, without any of the brain-rattling consequences. Unfortunately, a lot of these shots were done without any protection, with the skull absorbing the full force of the swung steel chair.

Those wrestlers who didn't put their hands up ended up having to deal with a myriad of concussions at the time, and the after effects of those injuries in the years to come - former ECW champion Mike Awesome being the case in point; in February 2007, barely a year after ending a 17-year career that was peppered with stiff chair shots to the head, Awesome took his own life at the age of just 42.

Sadly, it wasn't a one-off. In April 2010, Chris Kanyon - best known for his run in WCW and WWE - took his own life following a long, self-admitted battle with bipolar disorder and depression. A year later, Larry Sweeney, whose biggest break came as a manager with the independent Ring of Honor promotion (and playing the part of the fake Nick Hogan on an episode of Raw in July 2006) committed suicide, following a similar battle.

Regardless of the circumstances, whether the passing was expected or otherwise, or whether the deceased was a worldwide star or not, receiving "the call" is a nightmare. Having endured this experience myself, it's not pleasant. The name Adam Firestorm was not known worldwide to anywhere near the same level as Kanyon, Awesome or even Sweeney. Wrestling mainly in Western Canada and the North-West of America, Firestorm's in-ring career came to an end in 2005 after suffering an elbow injury. Although he did make a limited number of appearances at shows after then, Firestorm turned to life outside of the wrestling ring, focusing on a video production business, and later, co-hosting a podcast with myself. The last time I spoke to Adam was during the recording of a show, where he seemed his usual, happy self, showing zero signs of what was to happen in the coming hours. Going to bed after doing the recording on Wednesday night, Adam passed away a day later, and it wasn't until Friday night/Saturday morning when the news broke, courtesy of "the call".

It was a very rude awakening, on Saturday morning, in fact. Taking just a few short seconds, everything came crashing down, as the realisation hit hard: a close friend whom I spoke to pretty much every day was no longer going to be there. Although it was not on the same level as losing a friend you saw, travelled and worked with every day, the loss was hard to take - and still is. Although I have attended many wrestling shows across the world, and interviewed many stars, I have not stepped into the ring - and this was a rather blunt insight into the world that every wrestler eventually experiences.

Sadly, in wrestling's recent history, too many have had experience of "the call". In most of those cases, the end result of "the call" was avoidable. In hindsight, it really is a case of watching your favourites and realising that they have gone too soon.

Made in the USA
Lexington, KY
08 December 2012